SESAME STREET

All about VETERINARIANS

Susan B. Katz

Lerner Publications ◆ Minneapolis

Who are the people in your neighborhood?

Sesame Street has always been set smack in the middle of a friendly, busy community. We know that for all children, getting to know their communities is crucially important. So is understanding that everyone in the neighborhood—including kids!—has a part to play. In the *Sesame Street®* *Loves Community Helpers* books, *Sesame Street*'s favorite furry friends help young readers get to know some of these helpers better.

Sincerely,
The Editors at
Sesame Workshop

Broadview Public Library District

2226 S 16th Avenue

Broadview IL 60155-4000

708-345-1325

www.broadviewlibrary.org

Table of Contents

Veterinarians Are Wonderful!

Veterinarians are doctors that care for animals, like Elmo's puppy, Tango!

Why We Love Veterinarians

Veterinarians help our community by keeping animals healthy.

Veterinarians are sometimes called vets!

Veterinarians are caring, kind, and gentle people.

Vets love to help animals!

8

Veterinarians go to a special school. They study science and learn how to take care of animals.

Veterinarians know a lot about animals.

Animals visit veterinarians for checkups.
They also go to the veterinarian if they are sick.

Veterinarians check an animal's weight and temperature. They also listen to the animal's heart with a special tool called a stethoscope.

Doctors listen to my heart with a stethoscope too!

Veterinarians know what kind of food an animal should eat or how much exercise they should get.

Dogs can't eat chocolate. Me happy because that means more chocolate chip cookies for me!

17

Veterinarians also check an animal's body. They look inside the mouth and nose.

They also look inside an animal's ears.

19

Some veterinarians check and clean an animal's teeth.

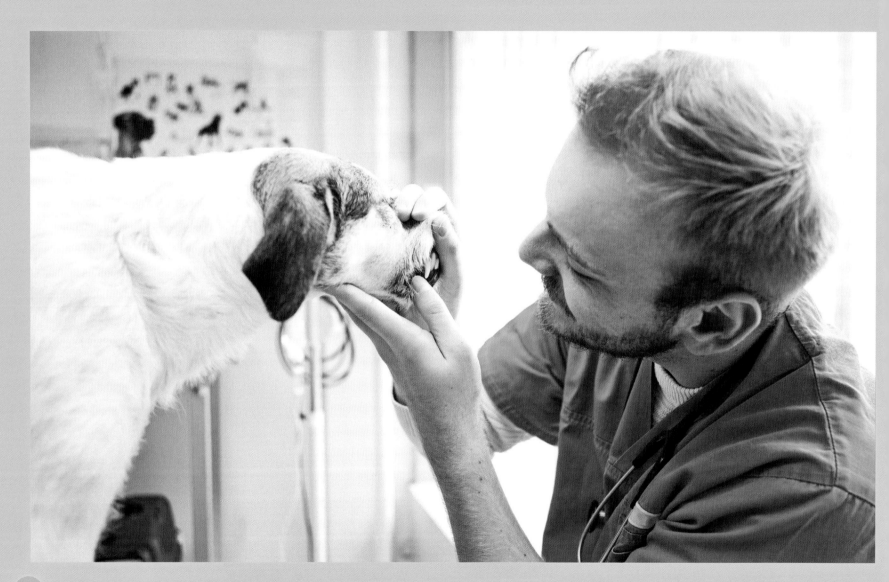

My rabbit, Harriet, needs chew toys to help keep her teeth healthy.

21

Some vets take care of large animals like horses and cows.

Vets can take care of animals that are as small as Slimey too!

Some veterinarians work in zoos. They take care of lions, tigers, and other animals.

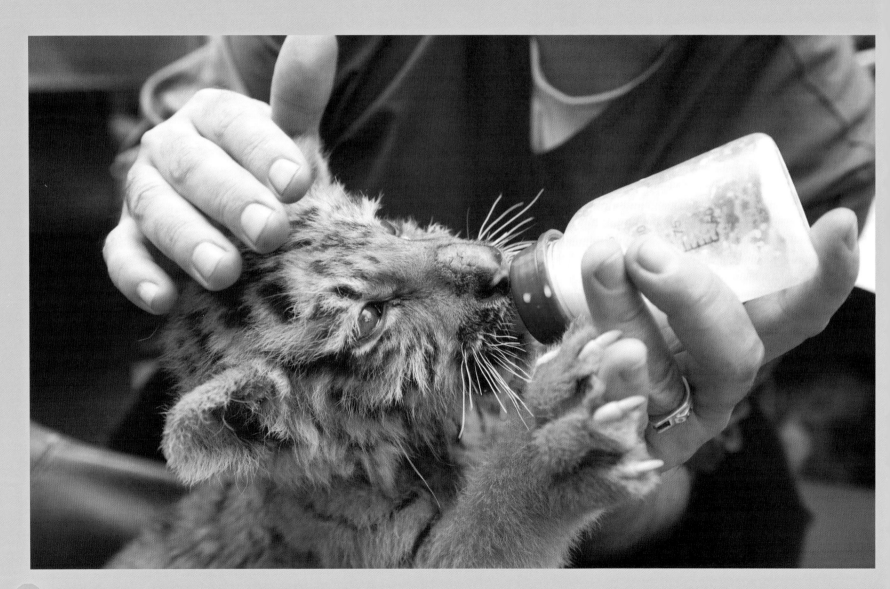

Veterinarians can answer questions that you have about your pet. Veterinarians always take good care of animals.

I bring my leopard gecko, Gary, to the veterinarian to make sure he stays healthy.

Thank You, Veterinarians!

You can be a helper too! Write a thank-you note to your veterinarian.

Dear Veterinarian,

Elmo loves how kind you are. Thank you for taking care of Tango and other animals.

Your friend,

Elmo

Picture Glossary

checkup: a visit to the vet to see if an animal is healthy

community: a place where people live and work

stethoscope: a tool used to listen to the heart and lungs

study: to learn

Read More

Ardely, Anthony. *I Can Be a Veterinarian*. New York: Gareth Stevens, 2019.

Peterson, Christy. *A Trip to the Zoo with Sesame Street*. Minneapolis: Lerner Publications, 2022.

Roberts, Antonia. *Veterinarians*. Minneapolis: Bearport, 2021.

Index

Photo Acknowledgments

Image credits: Serhii Bobyk/Shutterstock.com, p. 5; Rocketclips, Inc./Shutterstock.com, pp. 6, 30 (community); Fuse/Corbis/Getty Images, p. 7; Ariel Skelley/Getty Images, p. 8; Marko Geber/DigitalVision/Getty Images, p. 9; xavierarnau/E+/Getty Images, pp. 10, 30 (study); FatCamera/E+/Getty Images, p. 11; Kukurund/iStock/Getty Images, pp. 12, 30 (checkup); vitrolphoto/Shutterstock.com, p. 14; kali9/E+/Getty Images, pp. 15, 29, 30 (stethoscope); simonkr/E+/Getty Images, p. 16; Murilo Gualda/Getty Images, p. 18; bymuratdeniz/E+/Getty Images, p. 19; Nastasic/E+/Getty Images, p. 20; Martin Leigh/Photodisc/Getty Images, p. 21; Hauke-Christian Dittrich/picture-alliance/dpa/AP Images, p. 22; fotoedu/iStock/Getty Images, p. 23; zilli/iStock/Getty Images, p. 24; XiXinXing/Shutterstock.com, p. 26; Maria Sbytova/Shutterstock.com, p. 27.

Cover: hedgehog94/Shutterstock.com.

For Ginger, my dog from age 5 to 17, who was always there for me

Lerner Publications Company
An imprint of Lerner Publishing Group, Inc.
241 First Avenue North
Minneapolis, MN 55401 USA

For reading levels and more information, look up this title at www.lernerbooks.com.

Main body text set in Mikado Medium.
Typeface provided by HVD Fonts.

Editor: Brianna Kaiser
Lerner team: Martha Kranes

Library of Congress Cataloging-in-Publication Data

Names: Katz, Susan B., 1971- author.
Title: All about veterinarians / Susan B. Katz.
Description: Minneapolis : Lerner Publications, [2023] | Series: Sesame Street loves community helpers | Includes bibliographical references and index. | Audience: Ages 4–8 | Audience: Grades K–1 | Summary: "Veterinarians are valuable community helpers. Follow Sesame Street characters in learning how veterinarians help keep animals healthy and how they take care of animals big and small"— Provided by publisher.
Identifiers: LCCN 2021035573 | ISBN 9781728456126 (library binding) | ISBN 978-1-7284-6379-7 (paperback) | ISBN 978-1-7284-6215-8 (ebook)
Subjects: LCSH: Veterinarians—Juvenile literature.
Classification: LCC SF756 .K38 2023 | DDC 636.089092—dc23

LC record available at https://lccn.loc.gov/2021035573

Manufactured in the United States of America
1-50682-50101-12/10/2021